To hindy
Tons of love
    always.
From Anne & H!
      x x x

Flavia®

For information contact Powerfresh Limited
3 Gray Street, Northampton, NN1 3QQ
Telephone 0604 30996

ISBN: 0-8362-4705-1

A Place In
The Heart

Written and Illustrated
by Flavia Weedn

Kindness

is

born

from

a place

in the

heart...

a place

in a

gracious

heart.

Sometimes

when a

kindness is given

FLAVIA

it is

difficult

to express

our thanks...

because

its not

always

easy

FLAVIA

to

find

the right

words

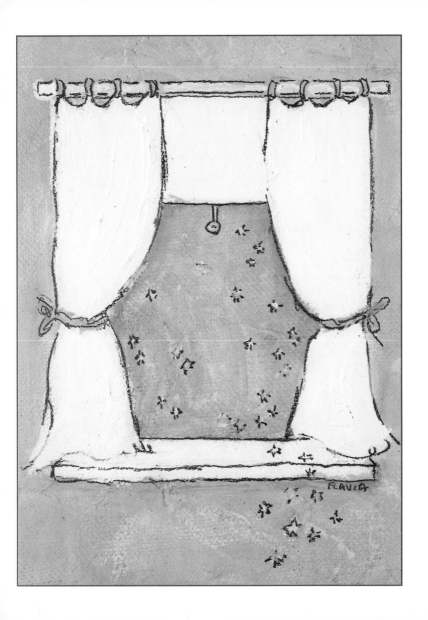

or

to know

just what

to say.

Maybe

its because the

words we need

are

so much

of what

we feel...

and maybe it's

because their

journey begins

FLAVIA

from

somewhere

far, far

away...

somewhere

in

the

heart.

FLAVIA

Thank

you.

Flavia at work in her Santa Barbara studio

Flavia Weedn is a writer, painter and philosopher.
Her life's work is about hope for the human spirit.
"I want to reach people of all ages who have never
been told, 'wait a minute, look around you. It's
wonderful to be alive and every one of us matters.
We can make a difference if we keep trying and
never give up.'" It is Flavia's and her family's wish
to awaken this spirit in each and every one of us.
Flavia's messages are translated into many foreign
languages on giftware, books and paper goods
around the world.

To find out more about Flavia write to:
Weedn Studios, Ltd.
740 State Street, 3rd Floor
Santa Barbara, CA 93101 USA
or call: 805-564-6909